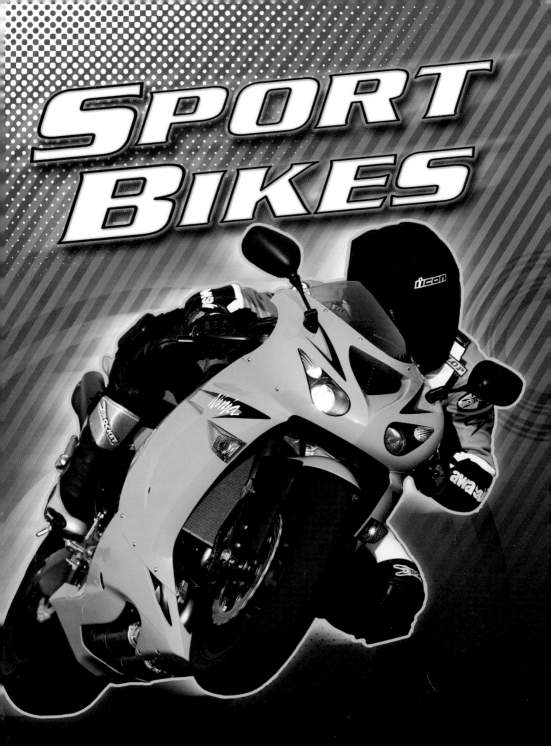

SPORT BIKES

BY JACK DAVID

BELLWETHER MEDIA · MINNEAPOLIS, MN

Are you ready to take it to the extreme?
Torque books thrust you into the action-packed
world of sports, vehicles, and adventure. These books
may include dirt, smoke, fire, and dangerous stunts.
WARNING: read at your own risk.

Library of Congress Cataloging-in-Publication Data

David, Jack, 1968-
  Sport bikes / by Jack David.
      p. cm. -- (Torque. Motorcycles)
  Includes bibliographical references and index.
  ISBN-13: 978-1-60014-135-5 (hbk. : alk. paper)
  ISBN-10: 1-60014-135-8 (hbk. : alk. paper)
  1. Motorcycles--Juvenile literature. 2. Motorcycles, Racing--Juvenile literature. I. Title.

  TL440.15.D3626 2008
  629.227'5--dc22
                                                                        2007014199

This edition first published in 2008 by Bellwether Media.

CONTENTS

A motorcycle speeds along a curvy mountain road. The rider leans forward over the handlebars of his Aprilia. The Aprilia is built for speed and control.

FAST FACT
THE KAWASAKI NINJA ZX-14 CAN ACCELERATE TO 62 MPH (100KM/H) FROM A DEAD STOP IN 2.5 SECONDS.

The rider approaches a curve. He leans his bike into the turn. The bike's tires grip the road as the bike leans at an angle. The rider's knee is only a foot above the road. The bike returns to an upright position as the road straightens. The engine hums as the rider speeds toward the next curve.

WHAT IS A SPORT BIKE?

Sport bikes are motorcycles built for **performance**. A motorcycle's performance is its speed, **acceleration**, and turning ability. Sport bikes are lightweight and fast. Their powerful engines give them great acceleration and awesome speeds. They can reach speeds of 200 miles (322 kilometers) per hour or faster. Sport bikes are built for riding on paved roads. They don't handle well on rough **terrain**.

Riders can choose from a variety of sport bikes. Super bikes and hyper sport bikes are among the most popular. Super bikes are lightweight bikes with large engines. They are very fast. Hyper sport bikes are even faster. They are the largest and most powerful sport bikes.

Some riders want more than speed and acceleration. They also want bikes that can travel long distances. Sport touring bikes are perfect for these riders. Sport touring bikes combine the features of sport bikes with the features of touring motorcycles. Touring motorcycles are built for comfort and storage space.

The engine is a sport bike's most important feature. Engines are measured in cubic centimeters (cc). Large engines are more powerful than smaller ones. Small sport bikes may have engines of about 600cc. Hyper sport bike engines can be 1,400cc or more. These huge engines can push bikes to incredible speeds.

FAST FACT

JAPANESE SPORT BIKE MANUFACTURERS AGREED TO LIMIT BIKE SPEEDS TO 186 MPH (300 KM/H) IN 2001.

Sport bikes are designed to be lightweight and **aerodynamic**. Aerodynamic means they cut easily through the air. Low handlebars and a slanted windshield help reduce **wind resistance**. Even the rider stays aerodynamic by riding in a tucked position.

THE SPORT BIKE MOTORCYCLE EXPERIENCE

Sport bike riders love speed. It doesn't matter if they are on a road or a racetrack. Riders get a rush of excitement from leaning into curves at top speeds and accelerating down straight roads.

FAST FACT

JOHN NOONAN SET THE LAND-SPEED RECORD ON A SIT-DOWN MOTORCYCLE WHEN HE RODE 259.393 MPH (417.453 KM/H).

Riding fast can be dangerous. Even experienced riders should always wear helmets and other safety gear. Wiping out at high speeds can be deadly even with the proper equipment. This is why good sport bike riders follow safety guidelines and ride smart.

GLOSSARY

acceleration–the rate at which something speeds up

aerodynamic–a description for an object that cuts easily through the air with little wind resistance

performance–a vehicle's combination of speed, acceleration, and handling

terrain–the natural surface features of the land

wind resistance–the drag caused by air pushing against a moving body; wind resistance slows down a motorcycle.

TO LEARN MORE

AT THE LIBRARY
Armentrout, David and Patricia Armentrout. *Sportbikes*. Vero Beach, Fla.: Rourke Pub., 2006.

Dayton, Connor. *Superbikes*. New York: PowerKids Press, 2007.

Hill, Lee Sullivan. *Motorcycles*. Minneapolis, Minn.: Lerner Publications Co., 2004.

ON THE WEB
Learning more about motorcycles is as easy as 1, 2, 3.

1. Go to www.factsurfer.com

2. Enter "motorcycles" into search box.

3. Click the "Surf" button and you will see a list of related web sites.

With factsurfer.com, finding more information is just a click away.

INDEX

The photographs in this book are reproduced through the courtesy of:
Kawasaki Motors Corporation, cover, pp. 1,17; Piaggio, pp. 4-5, 6, 7,
18-19; Yamaha Motor Corporation, pp. 9, 10-11, 12-13, 14, 15, 16
(top, bottom), 21.